ROYAL COURT

D1147319

Royal Court Theatre presents

THE COUNTRY

by **Martin Crimp**

First performed at the Royal Court Jerwood Theatre Downstairs,
Sloane Square, London, on 11 May 2000

faber and faber

THE COUNTRY

by **Martin Crimp**

Cast in order of appearance
Richard **Owen Teale**
Corinne **Juliet Stevenson**
Rebecca **Indira Varma**

Director **Katie Mitchell**
Designer **Vicki Mortimer**
Lighting Designer **Paule Constable**
Sound Designer **Gareth Fry**
Movement Director **Struan Leslie**
Casting Director **Lisa Makin**
Production Manager **Paul Handley**
Company Stage Manager **Cath Binks**
Stage Manager **Pamela Vision**
Deputy Stage Manager **Louise McDermott**
Assistant Stage Manager **Tamara Albachari**
Design Assistant **Jo Downs**
Costume Supervisor **Iona Kenrick**
Dialect Coach **Jeannette Nelson**
Company Voice Work **Patsy Rodenburg**

Royal Court Theatre wishes to thank the following for their help with this production:
Dr Berry Beaumont, Marjorie Albachar, Williams Medical Supplies. Magazines supplied by BBC Wildlife
Magazine and Wild About Animals. Wardrobe care by Persil and Comfort courtesy of Lever Brothers Ltd.

THE COMPANY

Martin Crimp (writer)
Plays
For the Royal Court: Attempts on her Life
(1997), The Treatment (1993, winner of the John
Whiting Award), No One Sees The Video
(1991).
Other plays include: The Misanthrope (1996,
Young Vic), Getting Attention (1992, West
Yorkshire Playhouse), Play with Repeats (1989),
Dealing with Clair (1988), Four Attempted Acts
(1996, Orange Tree).
Translations
For the Royal Court: The Chairs (1997,
co-production with Theatre de Complicite).
Other translations include: The Triumph of Love
(1999, Almeida), The Maids (1999, Young Vic),
Roberto Zucco (1997, RSC).
Resident Dramatist at the Royal Court, 1997.

Paule Constable (lighting designer)
For the Royal Court: Dublin Carol, The Weir,
The Glory of Living.
Other theatre includes: The Seagull, Tales from
Ovid, The Dispute, Uncle Vanya, Beckett Shorts,
The Mysteries (RSC); The Villains' Opera,
Darker Face of the Earth, Haroun and the Sea of
Stories, Caucasian Chalk Circle (RNT); Amadeus
(West End, Broadway, Olivier nomination); Les
Miserables (Tel Aviv); Playhouse Creatures (Old
Vic); More Grimms' Tales (Young Vic and New
York); four productions for Theatre de
Complicite including the Olivier nominated
Street of Crocodiles.
Opera includes: productions for the English
National Opera, Welsh National Opera, Scottish
Opera, Opera North, New Zealand International
Festival.

Gareth Fry (sound designer)
Theatre Includes: The Oresteia (RNT); Noise of
Time, Mnemonic, The Street of Crocodiles
(Theatre de Complicite); Holy Mothers
(Ambassadors); Oh What A Lovely War (RNT
national tour & Camden Roundhouse); The Lion,
the Witch and the Wardrobe (RSC Stratford).

Struan Leslie (movement director)
Theatre includes: The Oresteia (RNT); Easy
Virtue (Chichester Festival); The Maids (Young
Vic); Morphic Resonance (Donmar Warehouse);
Attempts On Her Life (Piccolo Teatro di
Milano); Vassa (Almeida at the Albery); The
Suppliants (Gate); A Midsummer Night's Dream
(Regents Park Outdoor Theatre); Merchant of
Venice (RSC and Barbican); Cyrano de Bergerac
(Swan Theatre, regional and West End);
Albertine in Five Times (BAC); Rhinoceros
(Riverside Studios).
Opera includes: Cosi Fan Tutti, Jenufa (Welsh
National Opera).
Forthcoming work includes: The Solemn Mass
for a Summer Full Moon (Traverse, Edinburgh).

Katie Mitchell (director)
Theatre includes: A Woman Killed With
Kindness, The Dybbuk, Ghosts, Henry VI,
Easter, Phoenician Woman, The Mysteries,
Beckett Shorts, Uncle Vanya (with The Young
Vic) (RSC); Rutherford and Son, The Machine
Wreckers, The Oresteia (RNT); The Last Ones
(Abbey Dublin); Endgame (Donmar
Warehouse); Attempts On Her Life (Piccolo
Teatro di Milano); The Maids (Young Vic).
Television includes: Widowing of Mrs Holroyd
(BBC Performance).
Opera includes: Don Giovanni and Jenufa
(Welsh National Opera).
Awards include: 1996 Evening Standard Award
for Best Director for The Phoenician Woman
(RSC).

Vicki Mortimer (designer)
Theatre includes: The Maids (Young Vic); The
Real Thing, The Seagull, A Woman Killed with
Kindness, The Dybbuk, Ghosts, Phoenician
Women, Beckett Shorts, Uncle Vanya, The
Creation, The Passion (RSC); The Oresteia,
Rutherford & Son, The Machine Wreckers, Fair
Ladies at a Game of Poem Cards, Closer
(RNT); 1953, Heartbreak House (Almeida);
Therese Raquin, 'Tis Pity She's a Whore, Hedda
Gabler, L'Aigle a Deux Tetes, The Changeling,
Three Sisters, Lady Aoi, Hanjo, Electra, Lulu,
The Triumph of Love (Theatre Project Tokyo).
Opera includes: Salome (ENO); Jenufa (Welsh
National Opera); The Turn of the Screw
(Scottish Opera).
Dance includes: Millenium, Sulpher 16, Aeon
(Random Dance Co.).

Juliet Stevenson

For the Royal Court: Death and the Maiden (also at Duke of Yorks), Other Worlds.
Other Theatre includes: Beckett Shorts, Not I, Footfalls, Les Liaisons Dangereuses, As You Like It, Troilus and Cressida, Measure for Measure, A Midsummer Night's Dream, The Witch of Edmonton, Money, Henry IV Parts I and II, Once in a Lifetime, The White Guard, Hippolytus, Anthony and Cleopatra, The Churchill Play, The Taming of the Shrew, The Tempest (RSC); Private Lives, Caucasian Chalk Circle, Hedda Gabler, Yerma (RNT); The Duchess of Malfi (Greenwich/West End); Scenes from an Execution (Mark Taper Forum LA); Burn This (Hampstead/West End); On the Verge (Sadlers Wells); The Trackers of Oxyrhynchus (National Studio).
Television includes: Trial by Fire, Cider with Rosie, Stone Scissors Paper, The Politician's Wife, The Doll's House, In the Border Country, Truly Madly Deeply, The March, Omnibus-Rape, Amy, Living with Dinosaurs, Cut of Love, Stanley, Life Story, Antigone, Freud, Bazaar and Rummage, The Mallens, Maybury, Oedipus at Colonus.
Film includes: Emma, A Secret Rapture, Who Dealt, The Trial, Ladder of Swords, Drowning by Numbers, Truly Madly Deeply.
Radio includes: Hangup, Whale Music, Cigarettes and Chocolate, A Little Like Drowning, To The Lighthouse, Hamlet, Cymbeline.
Awards include: Time Out Award for Best Actress (Death & The Maiden), Laurence Olivier Best Actress Award (Death & The Maiden), Emmy Award for Best Children's Film for Television (Living with Dinosaurs), LA Drama Critics' Circle Award for Best Actress (Scenes from an Execution).
Evening Standard Film Award for Best Actress (Truly Madly Deeply).

Owen Teale

Theatre includes: A Doll's House (West End and Broadway); Love's Labour's Lost, The Merchant of Venice, King Lear, Julius Caesar, Henry IV Part I (RSC); Berenice (RNT); Comedy of Errors (Bristol Old Vic); When She Danced (King's Head); The Fifteen Streets (Belgrade Coventry and West End); Macbeth (Clywd Theatr Cymru).
Television includes: Belonging, Ballykissangel, Love in the House of Our Lord, Wilderness, Dangerfield, Death of a Salesman, Thin Blue Line, Dangerous Lady, The Secret House of Death, The Vacillations of Poppy Carew, The Fifteen Streets, Great Expectations, Strife, Way Out of Order, David Copperfield.
Film Includes: Cleopatra, The Cherry Orchard, La Guerre Des Moutons, Marco Polo, The Hawk, Robin Hood, War Requiem.
Awarded a Tony for his role in the production of A Doll's House on Broadway.

Indira Varma

Theatre includes: Celebration (Almeida); Three Sisters (Oxford Stage Co.); Othello (RNT); As You Like It (Nottingham Play House).
Television includes: Sci-Fright, In the Land of Plenty, Courage, Psychos, The Grove, Other People's Children.
Film includes: Dope Opera, Jinnah, Clancy's Kitchen, Kama Sutra, Sixth Happiness, My Indian Summer.
Radio includes: Moonlight, My Beating Heart, Naniji.

THE ENGLISH STAGE COMPANY
AT THE ROYAL COURT

The English Stage Company at the Royal Court opened in 1956 as a subsidised theatre producing new British plays, international plays and some classical revivals.

The first artistic director George Devine aimed to create a writers' theatre, 'a place where the dramatist is acknowledged as the fundamental creative force in the theatre and where the play is more important than the actors, the director, the designer'. The urgent need was to find a contemporary style in which the play, the acting, direction and design are all combined. He believed that 'the battle will be a long one to continue to create the right conditions for writers to work in'.

Devine aimed to discover 'hard-hitting, uncompromising writers whose plays are stimulating, provocative and exciting'. The Royal Court production of John Osborne's Look Back in Anger in May 1956 is now seen as the decisive starting point of modern British drama, and the policy created a new generation of British playwrights. The first wave included John Osborne, Arnold Wesker, John Arden, Ann Jellicoe, N F Simpson and Edward Bond. Early seasons included new international plays by Bertolt Brecht, Eugène Ionesco, Samuel Beckett, Jean-Paul Sartre and Marguerite Duras.

The theatre started with the 400-seat proscenium arch Theatre Downstairs, and then in 1969 opened a second theatre, the 60-seat studio Theatre Upstairs. Productions in the Theatre Upstairs have transferred to the West End, such as Conor McPherson's The Weir, Kevin Elyot's My Night With Reg and Ariel Dorfman's Death and the Maiden. The Royal Court also co-produces plays which have transferred to the West End or toured internationally, such as Sebastian Barry's The Steward of Christendom and Mark Ravenhill's Shopping and Fucking (with Out of Joint), Martin McDonagh's The Beauty Queen Of Leenane (with Druid Theatre Company), Ayub Khan-Din's East is East (with Tamasha Theatre Company, and now a feature film).

Since 1994 the Royal Court's artistic policy has again been vigorously directed to finding a new generation of playwrights. The writers include Joe Penhall, Rebecca Prichard, Michael Wynne, Nick Grosso, Judy Upton, Meredith Oakes, Sarah Kane, Anthony Neilson, Judith Johnson, James Stock, Jez Butterworth, Simon Block, Martin McDonagh, Mark Ravenhill, Ayub Khan-Din, Tamantha Hammerschlag, Jess Walters, Conor McPherson, Simon Stephens, Richard

Bean, Roy Williams, Gary Mitchell, Mick Mahoney, Rebecca Gilman, Christopher Shinn and Kia Corthron. This expanded programme of new plays has been made possible through the support of the Jerwood Foundation and the American Friends of the Royal Court Theatre, and many in association with the Royal National Theatre Studio.

In recent years there have been record-breaking productions at the box office, with capacity houses for Jez Butterworth's Mojo, Sebastian Barry's The Steward of Christendom, Martin McDonagh's The Beauty Queen of Leenane, Ayub Khan-Din's East is East, Eugène Ionesco's The Chairs and Conor McPherson's The Weir, which transferred to the West End in October 1998 and is now running at the Duke of York's Theatre.

The newly refurbished theatre in Sloane Square opened in February 2000, with a policy still inspired by the first artistic director George Devine. The Royal Court is an international theatre for new plays and new playwrights, and the work shapes contemporary drama in Britain and overseas.

AWARDS FOR
THE ROYAL COURT

Ariel Dorfman's Death and the Maiden and John Guare's Six Degrees of Separation won the Olivier Award for Best Play in 1992 and 1993 respectively. Terry Johnson's Hysteria won the 1994 Olivier Award for Best Comedy, and also the Writers' Guild Award for Best West End Play. Kevin Elyot's My Night with Reg won the 1994 Writers' Guild Award for Best Fringe Play, the Evening Standard Award for Best Comedy, and the 1994 Olivier Award for Best Comedy. Joe Penhall was joint winner of the 1994 John Whiting Award for Some Voices. Sebastian Barry won the 1995 Writers' Guild Award for Best Fringe Play, the 1995 Critics' Circle Award and the 1997 Christopher Ewart-Biggs Literary Prize for The Steward of Christendom, and the 1995 Lloyds Private Banking Playwright of the Year Award. Jez Butterworth won the 1995 George Devine Award for Most Promising Playwright, the 1995 Writers' Guild New Writer of the Year Award, the Evening Standard Award for Most Promising Playwright and the 1995 Olivier Award for Best Comedy for Mojo. Phyllis Nagy won the 1995 Writers' Guild Award for Best Regional Play for Disappeared.

The Royal Court was the overall winner of the 1995 Prudential Award for the Arts for creativity, excellence, innovation and accessibility. The Royal Court Theatre Upstairs won the 1995 Peter Brook Empty Space Award for innovation and excellence in theatre.

Michael Wynne won the 1996 Meyer-Whitworth Award for The Knocky. Martin McDonagh won the 1996 George Devine Award, the 1996 Writers' Guild Best Fringe Play Award, the 1996 Critics' Circle Award and the 1996 Evening Standard Award for Most Promising Playwright for The Beauty Queen of Leenane. Marina Carr won the 19th Susan Smith Blackburn Prize (1996/7) for Portia Coughlan. Conor McPherson won the 1997 George Devine Award, the 1997 Critics' Circle Award and the 1997 Evening Standard Award for Most Promising Playwright for The Weir. Ayub Khan-Din won the 1997 Writers' Guild Award for Best West End Play, the 1997 Writers' Guild New Writer of the Year Award and the 1996 John Whiting Award for East is East. Anthony Neilson won the 1997 Writers' Guild Award for Best Fringe Play for The Censor.

At the 1998 Tony Awards, Martin McDonagh's The Beauty Queen of Leenane (co-production with Druid Theatre Company) won four awards including Garry Hynes for Best Director and was nominated for a further two. Eugene Ionesco's The Chairs (co-production with Theatre de

Complicite) was nominated for six Tony awards. David Hare won the 1998 Time Out Live Award for Outstanding Achievement for Via Dolorosa. Sarah Kane won the 1998 Arts Foundation Fellowship in Playwriting. Rebecca Prichard won the 1998 Critics' Circle Award for Most Promising Playwright for Yard Gal.

Conor McPherson won the 1999 Olivier Award for Best New Play for The Weir. The Royal Court won the 1999 ITI Award for Excellence in International Theatre. Sarah Kane's Cleansed was judged Best Foreign Language Play in 1999 by Theater Heute in Germany. Gary Mitchell won the 1999 Pearson Best Play Award for Trust. Rebecca Gilman was joint winner of the 1999 George Devine Award and won the 1999 Evening Standard Award for Most Promising Playwright for The Glory of Living.

In 1999, the Royal Court won the European theatre prize New Theatrical Realities, presented at Taormina Arte in Sicily, for its efforts in recent years in discovering and producing the work of young British dramatists.

ROYAL COURT BOOKSHOP

The bookshop offers a wide range of playtexts, theatre books, screenplays and art-house videos with over 1,000 titles.

Located in the downstairs BAR AND FOOD area, the bookshop is open Monday to Saturday, daytimes and evenings.

Many of the Royal Court Theatre playtexts are available for just £2 including the plays in the current season and recent works by Conor McPherson, Martin Crimp, Caryl Churchill, Sarah Kane, David Mamet, Phyllis Nagy and Rebecca Prichard. We offer a 10% reduction to students on a range of titles.

Further information : 020 7565 5024

REBUILDING THE ROYAL COURT

In 1995, the Royal Court was awarded a National Lottery grant through the Arts Council of England, to pay for three quarters of a £26m project to rebuild completely our 100-year old home. The rules of the award required the Royal Court to raise £7.5m in partnership funding. The building has been completed thanks to the generous support of those listed below. We are particularly grateful for the contributions of over 5,700 audience members.

If you would like to support the ongoing work of the Royal Court please contact the Development Department on 020 7565 5000.

PROGRAMME SUPPORTERS

The Royal Court (English Stage Company Ltd) receives its principal funding from the London Arts Board. It is also supported financially by a wide range of private companies and public bodies and earns the remainder of its income from the box office and its own trading activities. The Royal Borough of Kensington & Chelsea gives an annual grant to the Royal Court Young Writers' Programme and the London Boroughs Grants Committee provides project funding for a number of play development initiatives.

Royal Court Registered Charity number 231242.

This year the Jerwood Charitable Foundation continues to support new plays by new playwrights with the fifth series of Jerwood New Playwrights. Since 1993 the A.S.K. Theater Projects of Los Angeles has funded a Playwrights' Programme at the theatre. Bloomberg Mondays, a continuation of the Royal Court's reduced price ticket scheme, is supported by Bloomberg News. BSkyB has also generously committed to a two-year sponsorship of the Royal Court Young Writers' Festival.

FOR THE ROYAL COURT

We put more into our programmes, too.

Carlton Television. Producing and broadcasting programmes that live up to the highest standards. Yours.

The Country

First published in 2000
by Faber and Faber Limited
3 Queen Square London WC1N 3AU

Photoset by Faber and Faber Ltd
Printed in England by Mackays of Chatham plc, Chatham, Kent

A CIP record for this book
is available from the British Library

ISBN 0-571-20340-X

2 4 6 8 10 9 7 5 3 1

Characters

Corinne, forty
Richard, forty
Rebecca, twenty-five

Corinne and Richard are from London.
Rebecca is American.

Time
The present

Place
The country

Note
A slash (/) marks the point of interruption
in overlapping dialogue.

I

Interior. Night.
   A large room, wooden chairs, an old table.
   Richard and Corinne.

— What are you doing?

— I'm cutting.

— What are you cutting?

— I don't know . . . I'm making something. Why are you looking at me like that?

— You don't normally cut. You don't normally make things. What are you making?

— I just thought I'd cut out some pictures to go round the cot. I thought they'd be stimulating.

— Are they bright?

— Some of them are bright.

   She cuts.

   Some of them are just pictures.

— It's a good idea.

— D'you think it's a good idea? I'm not sure if it's a good idea.

— Have you got enough light?

— Oh, I've got plenty of light. Thank you.

She cuts.

This . . . person. Is she asleep? When will she wake up?

— Don't hurt your eyes.

— Is she alive?

— Well of course she's alive. What sort of question / is that?

— Well I don't know, do I. I don't know if she's alive.

— Of course she's alive. She's asleep.

— Did you give her something?

— Something what?

— Something to make her.

— Not to make her but to help her.

— Not to make her but to help her. Is there a difference?

— No.

Both faint laugh.

— Because why did you bring her here? Why ever did you bring her here?

— It's my job to bring her here.

— What? Into our house? In the middle of the night?

— Yes.

— Is it?

— Yes.

— Your *job*? It's your job to bring a strange woman into our house in the middle of the night?

— As I understand it.

— And *what* was she doing?

— I've told you what she was doing.

   Pause.

   D'you want something to drink?

— Lying there.

— Yes. Do you?

— Lying on the road.

— She was next to it.

— What? Sprawled? Sprawled next to it?

— (*shrugs*) If you like.

— Partying then.

— What?

— She'd been partying.

— I've no idea. She was incoherent.

— What? Completely incoherent? What sort of party *was* it? I'm glad she's not mine.

— Your what?

— My child. I'm glad she's not my child.

— She's not a child.

— Someone must love her, though.

— Why?

— Someone must.

   He moves to go out.

   I don't want alcohol.

— I'll get you some water.

He goes out.
She cuts.

— Have you called Morris?

— (*off*) What?

— Have you called Morris? Shouldn't he be informed?

— (*off*) Morris?

— Shouldn't you inform him?

— (*off*) He'll be asleep.

— D'you think he sleeps, then?

— (*off*) What?

He reappears with glass of water.

What?

— I can't imagine Morris asleep. (*Takes water.*) Thank you. I imagine him . . . alert, somehow. Permanently alert.

She sips.

— D'you think I should call him?

— It's just that you don't seem concerned.

— Well that's my job.

— Your job is not to be concerned?

— My job is not to seem it.

— Taste this.

— What?

— Taste it.

4

He sips the water.

— I can't taste anything.

— But there's a taste of something.

— What?

— Something . . . I don't know . . . purity. D'you think it's safe?

— It's water, that's all. It's a glass of water.

— But shouldn't there be something in it?

— It's just a glass of water.

— That's what I'm saying.

— It's water – it's pure – and so perhaps it has a taste.

— You can taste it then?

— I can't taste anything. It has no taste. It tastes of nothing. But perhaps that taste of nothing is what you can taste.

— You can't then?

— No, I can't. I'm sorry.

— You drink it.

— Don't you want it?

— No. You drink it.

He drinks all the water.
Pause.
She begins to laugh.

— What is it?

— The look on your face.

— What look on my face?

— When you appeared. The look on your face when you appeared with her in your arms.

— Oh? What was I doing?

— Smiling.

— What at?

— Well that's just it: you were standing there with this girl in your arms, smiling. And I thought: oh look, he's lost his sense of humour. He's finally lost his famous sense / of humour.

— But in fact you were wrong.

— In fact I was wrong.

— In fact my famous sense of humour survives intact.

— In fact your famous sense of humour does – yes – survive / intact.

— Because I think you should tell me. I think you should tell me if you feel I've done something wrong.

— No no no, what you've . . .

— Thank you.

— What you've . . . Wrong? No. Of course not.

— Thank you. / Good.

— What you've done is . . . What you've done is exactly what someone *would have done*.

— People can't be left.

— Well that's right.

— Can they?

— I don't think that they *can*, no. Clearly they *can't*.

— This isn't the city.

— I know.

— This isn't the city, you can't just . . .

— I know you can't.

   Pause.

   So there wasn't a bag?

— A what?

— A bag. A purse. Didn't she have some kind of . . .

— A purse?

— Yes. A purse. A bag. Whatever. Don't look so / blank.

— Why do you say that: purse?

— Why do I say it?

— Yes. Why do you say it when it's not English?

— What is not English?

— Purse is not English.

— I'm not speaking English?

— Of course you're speaking / English.

— Well did she?

— What? Sorry?

— Have one.

— Have a bag?

— Did she?

— I'm not . . .

— You're not sure.

— No.

— You didn't . . .

— No.

— You didn't look.

— No. For a bag? No. Why?

— 'Why'?

— Yes.

— *What?*

Pause.

What? Because if there was a bag . . .

— I know.

— If there was a bag . . .

— Yes – only the light was going . . .

— . . . then we could look – couldn't we – in the bag and
it might . . . / simplify things. We wouldn't be . . .

— I've told you: the light was going. The imperative was
to get her off that road and to ensure her safety. The
bag was not – yes, it would simplify things – but the
bag was not, as I'm sure you can imagine, uppermost
in my mind.

— The bag.

— What?

— So there was a bag.

— I don't know if there was a bag.

— If there was a bag, you should go back. You should go
back and look for it.

— D'you want me to go back and look for it? If you want me to go back and look for it, I'll go back and look for it.

— No, I don't want you to go back and look for it, I want you to kiss me.

— I don't want to kiss you. I *have* kissed you.

— Then kiss me again.

— I don't want to kiss you again.

— Why? Don't you love me?

Pause.

— What?

— You don't have to look so blank. I said: don't you / love me?

— I don't want to kiss you. I don't feel clean.

— Well you look clean.

— I don't feel it.

— Then take a shower. Take a shower, and when you're clean come back and kiss me.

— I'll wake the children up.

— I don't think you will wake the children up.

— How have they been?

— Oh, sweet.

Pause.

I took them to Sophie's, actually. I left them at Sophie's for the afternoon. I had a whole afternoon free. Sophie's so kind.

9

— I hope you gave her something.

— I always give her something. In fact I always give her far too much. As if she were poor.

— She is poor.

— Sophie? I didn't know she was poor.

— Everyone knows she's poor.

— But she's so neat. And her house is so neat. It's so clean. She has flowers in the kitchen. What d'you mean, 'she's poor'?

— She has no money.

— She has a house.

— The house is collapsing. It isn't hers. She's a tenant.

— I don't believe you. I don't believe Sophie's poor. She can't be.

— That cup she puts the money in? Well all the money she has at any time is in that cup.

Pause.

— Well don't you want to hear what I did with my afternoon?

Pause.

I'll tell you what I did, then.

— What did you do?

— I took one of these old chairs and I sat under a tree.

— That sounds nice.

— It was lovely.

Pause.

— Which tree was that?

— The one by the stream.

— The alder.

— Is that the alder?

— The one by the stream / is, yes.

— Well whatever it is, I sat under it. Sat under it for so long in fact that the back legs sank into the moss. And I just looked at the land. I sat there and I just looked out at the land.

Pause.

— And how was the land?

— It was lovely. The land was lovely. All the hills were rolling and all the clouds were unravelling, like in a fairy-tale. I felt like that girl in the fairy-tale. Who's that girl in the fairy-tale?

— A goat-girl.

— A goat-girl or something. I felt – that's right – just like a goat-girl, only without the goats thankfully. And I thought of you driving, with your sense of humour, which I felt sure you would need, along all those country lanes to visit the sick and so on, and I can't tell you how happy I felt, how good it all felt. Which is when Morris appeared.

— What did *Morris* want?

— Well that's what *I* said. I said, 'What can I do for you, Morry?' He said, 'I see you're making yourself quite at home.' I said, 'Well this *is* my home now, Morry.' He said, 'I'm sorry if I'm disturbing you, I was looking for Richard.' I said, 'Richard's not here, I'm afraid. Presumably he's out doing the rounds.' And

Morris said, 'Yes. That must be it.'

Pause.

— I hope you were nice to him.

— I was incredibly nice to him. Even when he squatted right next to me in his terrible tweeds.

— Oh god, not the terrible tweeds.

— He squatted right next to me – yes – and asked how we were settling in.

— What did he mean by that?

— He just asked how we were settling in. Did we miss the city?

— And did we?

— What? Miss the city? Well *I* didn't. I told him I couldn't speak for you.

— Did he expect you to speak for me?

— I don't know what he expected. He said he was on his way to the DIY superstore to buy some paint, and did we need anything?

— Paint?

— Yes. Apparently he has little posts lining his driveway and every year he paints them.

— Doesn't he have any paint at home?

— Well that's what I said. I said, 'Don't you have any paint at home?' And no, he doesn't. Or rather, yes, he does. He does have some paint at home – it's the paint he used last time he painted the posts – only he doesn't know where it is.

Pause.

— So someone's moved the pot.

— No, he thinks he's moved the pot himself. He feels sure he moved the pot, but he doesn't remember where. I said, 'That must be very frustrating for you, Morry.' But the thing is, is then he began to talk to me in another language. One moment it was English – the paint and so on – then the next it was like he was chanting to me in another language. I said, 'What's that, Morry?' And of course I couldn't help laughing. He said, 'It's Latin. It's Virgil.'

— Virgil.

— Well that's what *I* said. I said, '*Virgil*, Morris? You make me feel so ignorant.' And he did. He was making me feel very very ignorant. Squatting there. Chanting like that.

— Surely not. Surely he meant well.

— Well no, I don't think that he did. I don't think that he did 'mean well'. I kept thinking, 'Why have you come here? What do you want?'

— And what *did* he want?

— Well that's what I kept wondering. He said it was about bees. That seeing me sitting like that next to a stream brought it back to him.

— Brought what back to him?

— This thing. This . . . poem.

— Christ.

— Yes. And it's just that I can't help thinking, what if it had been a man? (*faint laugh*) Don't look so blank. I'm just wondering – if it – she – if she had been a man, would you have been so . . . (*Shrugs.*) That's all.

13

— A man.

— Would you still have been so – a man, yes – so solicitous?

— 'Would I still have been so solicitous'?

— Well *would* you? *Would* you – if instead of . . .

— Solicitous.

— Yes. If instead of some frail young . . . slim young . . .
abandoned at the / side of a road.

— What d'you mean, / 'solicitous'?

— If instead of this . . . vision, this victim of some unspec-
ified, some undiagnosed . . . misfortune, let's say it had
been some man you had found, some man perhaps
crawling out of a ditch with his clothes covered in
muck . . .

— No one – I'm sorry – but no one was crawling / out of
any ditch.

— Well all right then – not crawling, but unconscious.
You round the bend and instead of that, that . . . person, it's a man who's drunk himself into a stupor and
he's lying there in his own sick and he's wet himself.
Would you really have lifted this man into your car?
Would you have driven him all this way to your own
house where your children are sleeping?

She resumes cutting.

That's all I meant by solicitous.

— I can't help what sex she is.

— Well obviously.

— And besides, she hasn't been sick. She hasn't wet herself.

14

— So far as you know.

— So far as I know.

— *Do* you know?

— What?

— *Do* you know?

She accidentally cuts herself with the scissors – sucks her finger – looks at him.

— Well yes, it's my job, isn't it, as a matter of fact, to know.
    What have you done?

— Oh. Nothing. Cut myself.

— Is it deep? Does it hurt? Wash it.

— I'd rather suck it.

— Well suck it then.

They both laugh.
    He moves away.

— Where are you going?

— I'm going to take that shower.

He goes out.
    She squeezes her finger, looks at the blood.

(. . . scissors)

II

The same scene, a few minutes later.
    Corinne, alone, has a small object pressed to her ear.
    Richard appears, doing up his shirt, watching her.
    She dangles the object – a wrist-watch – by its thin
gold bracelet, and smiles to herself.*

— Why did you do that?

— It's her watch.

— I know it's her watch. Give it to me, please.

— To you?

— Yes.

    She closes it in her fist.
       They both smile.

— I wanted to touch her.

— Why did you want to touch her?

— To see if she was hot.

— And was she?

— What?

— Hot.

— I uncovered her.

— You're not to uncover her.

    Pause.

    Why did you uncover her?

— I was curious about her arms, actually. Have you looked at her arms?

— No, I haven't looked at her arms.

— Her legs, then. Have you looked at her face? Haven't you looked at her? Haven't you looked at any part of her?

Pause.

Aren't you curious?

— I'd like you to give me the watch. I'd like you to stop clutching it. Why are you clutching it like that?

— I'm not clutching it, I'm holding it in my hand.

— You'll damage it.

Pause.
  She holds the watch out to him.

— It's beautiful. It shows the phases of the moon.

As he gets close and reaches for the watch, she snaps it back in her fist.

But first you have to kiss me.

— I have kissed you.

— Then you have to kiss me again.

She slowly opens her fist. He comes closer, he takes the watch, she grips his hand, the phone rings.
  They don't move.

Leave it.

— I can't leave it. You know I can't leave it.

He pulls his hand away and answers the phone.

Yes? Hello?

(*brightly*) Morris. (It's Morris.) Yes. Sorry.

It's not, of course it's not late.

No, Morris, we were just, we were just, we were just . . .

— Here.

— We were just *here*. We were just enjoying the –

Well that's right: the evening, the beautiful evening. Did you see that sky, that fabulous sky?

Well yes, I *mean* earlier on. It *was* earlier on. It's dark now, of course it is – though quite starry, I should imagine.

Starry – as in bright – with stars.

Well I'll tell her, I'll certainly tell her, Morris. (He got the paint.) Yes, she'll be pleased to know that.

You *didn't*?

Oh *really*? (*Chuckles.*)

(He found the other pot when he got back home.) So now you've got two, Morris.

I said: so / now you've got –

— Just tell him to go away.

— (What?)

— Tell him to leave us alone. Tell him to / go away.

— Well what an extraordinary place to find it. Listen, Morry . . . what if I were to call you back in the morning. Because the thing is, is we . . .

(*seriously*) Uh-huh, uh-huh, uh-huh.

Well how did that –

Uh-huh. Well how did that –

Uh-huh, uh-huh, uh-huh.

Well how did that *happen*? (Can you get me something to write with?)

Nothing, nothing, I just said how did it happen, Morris? When was this?

19

— What?

— Excuse me. (A pencil. Something to write with.) So when exactly was this?

Corinne goes out.

Uh-huh, uh-huh.

   Well hang on a minute, Morris, hang on a minute. Because the fact is, is (a) I fully intended to make that visit, and (b) regardless of any visit the man was always going to die. This was a sick old man, Morris. You've been there. You've seen that house. You've seen him trying to breathe. You know his history. And please don't let's forget that the man was a bastard.

   Difficult? He was a manipulative old bastard, Morris, as you well know.

Corinne returns with a pencil. She also brings a woman's bag – a handbag or miniature backpack.

I take your point, I absolutely take your point. Of course it doesn't look good, but that doesn't necessarily mean it 'looks bad'. It doesn't necessarily mean it *is* bad. Because it's simply a thing, Morris (thank you), simply a thing, a thing that – unfortunately – yes – happens.

   Well yes, I did intend to visit. Obviously. The visit was noted.

— Ask him / about the girl.

— The visit was noted. The intention to visit was noted. (What?)

— Ask him about –

— Excuse me, Morris. (What?)

— Ask him about the girl. Tell him she's in pain.

Pause.

Well tell him.

— (Of course she's not in pain. She's asleep.) Morris? No.
Nothing. Just a little / domestic –

— Then why does she take pain-killers? Why does she
have / needles?

— Just a little domestic . . . (please . . .) (*He gestures to
be left alone.*) . . . Sorry. Yes. Of course I'm listening,
Morry. It was just a little domestic (shit, fuck) no,
nothing, I'm just getting myself tangled, Morris, in this
flex. The phone here is something out of a *museum* . . .
you have to rotate the . . .
    That's right: the dial. Now listen, Morris, I'm
assuming I have your support –
    What? No no no, of course I don't, of course I don't
feel 'accused'. (*Laughs.*) I know you just have to establish – which you are – which you have – the facts, the
relevant facts. And then the two of us simply have to
present –
    Well of course I'm not expecting you to lie, Morris.
No one has to lie. That wouldn't be appropriate. It's
simply a matter of putting these events in some kind of
order, some kind of intelligible order.
    Okay, we'll talk again, let's talk again, Morris, in the
morning.
    Goodnight. (*He hangs up.*)

— What's happened?

— Nothing's happened. Where did you find that?

— Where did I find this?

— Where did you find that? Yes.

— I found it in your car. I found it under the seat. You

obviously *did* pick it up. It didn't sound like you not to have picked it up, and there it was.

— Uh-huh.

— (*faint laugh*) Yes.

— You looked.

— Yes. Of course I looked. I looked / under the seat.

— You looked for the bag.

— Yes, I looked for the bag. I not only looked for the bag, I found the bag. Here is the bag.

She gently empties the contents of the bag on to the floor. Pause.

It's just that I suddenly feel, I suddenly feel – help me – I suddenly feel lost. I don't know who you are. I don't know what you want. Because I thought you'd stopped. But if you've stopped why are there needles in her bag? Whose needles are they? Did she *pay* you for these things? *How* did she pay you?

Pause.

Who is she? Have you any idea? You probably don't even know / her name.

— She got into the car, that's all.

— I see.

— She just got into the car.

— I see. She just got into the car.

— Exactly.

— And why was that?

— Why?

— Yes, why was that?

— To see a stone.

— To see a stone. She got into your car to see a stone.

— Yes.

— What stone?

— I've no idea what stone. Now put her things back into the bag. Don't touch her things. There's no reason to touch her things. She's asleep. Let her sleep. In the morning she'll wake up. And she'll leave.

Pause.

(*ending the story*) And this is what happened.

— What is what happened?

— This is. This is exactly all that happened. Don't look at / me like that.

— I thought you'd stopped. I thought that was the point of / *coming* here.

— Now put her things back please into the bag.

— Does Morris know?

— Of course he doesn't know.

— Get her out of here.

— How can I get her / out of here?

— Take her to Morris.

— Of course. Take her to Morris. 'Oh, good evening, Morris. I found this young woman unconscious on the track after shooting up in my Peugeot and I'd just like to get a second opinion.' 'Just the ticket, old boy. Wheel her into the library and sample a fine old malt while we discuss the imminent termination of your career and subsequent life of shame and / poverty.'

— What 'track'?

— What?

— What 'track'? What d'you mean, 'she got into the car'?

— Take her to Morris. Yes.

— What d'you mean, 'she got into the car'? When did she get into the car? Is that why Morris appeared?

— Why Morris appeared?

— Why he appeared. Why he asked where you were.

— Listen: I can't lie to you.

— You *have* lied to me. The *track*? You have already / lied to me.

— I'm trying to explain this.

— What track?

— I don't know. A track, a track, a track such as you find. *Such as one simply finds.* (*softly*) It was on the map. It was her idea. *She* got into the car. And I refuse to be blamed – not by you – not by Morris. All right, so I cancelled the visits, but the visits are of no importance. I know those people, they pick up the phone and it's doctor this doctor that just so I can give them a scrip for something they could buy themselves from

— Why did she get into your car? I thought you'd found her by the road but now she's getting

24

into your car, you're driving along a track. She's complicit. Are you saying she's complicit – or what? – that you . . . Listen to me. What exactly are you saying, Richard? Well? What *difference*? What difference?

Boots the fucking Chemists. Chest pains, chest pains. Well of course he had chest pains. The man was eighty years old. What *difference* could it possibly make?

To bring this . . . person here while your children are asleep. To have me look for this bag. To *worry* about you. To crawl about in the dark under the car-seat like an idiot while you're – what – washing off the smell?

— Please.

— Washing off the smell, are you, and asking me what difference it makes?

— Please: this is not helpful.

— Oh really? What is helpful, then? To pick up girls? To entice them into your car? To drive them up / a *track*? What?

The phone rings.

— Nobody was enticed. Don't speak like that. That's not what this is about. Listen / to me.

— Then what *is* this about? Enlighten me. *Yes.*

Silence.
  The phone continues to ring on and on.
  Finally Richard answers it.

— Hello? (*brightly*) Morris.

Corinne leaves the room.

No no. I'm here. Definitely here.

25

Uh-huh. Uh-huh. Oblivious. How long has it been ringing, then? Because we were both completely obliv–

Not a problem, of course it's not a problem, only . . . only . . . I don't suppose there's any question of *you* doing this one, is there?

Corinne appears in the doorway, observing him.

Yup yup yup. Calm . . . Okay . . . Just calm down, Morris, and give me –

Yes. All right. Sorry. Give me the details.

Yup . . . yup . . . yup . . . got it. Tell them I'll be there in – what – twenty minutes.

Fifteen then. Fifteen. I will try my best to be there in fifteen minutes.

Well I do understand the urgency, Morry. Of course I understand the urgency. (*He hangs up.*)

He goes out, immediately returns with case, places it on table, pops open the lid, checks contents, snaps it shut.
      Pause.

— And if she wakes up?

Pause.

— What?

— And if she / wakes up?

— She's not going to wake up. Trust me.

He goes out rapidly.
      Corinne remains in the doorway.

(. . . stone)

III

Same scene, later.
Rebecca sits on a chair with a blanket over her shoulders. Corinne watches her speak.

— The sun was shining. The trees were green, but each green was different. I mean the green of each species was a different green.

Pause.

And I'd found the stone. Yes. This . . . outpost . . . of the empire. Only it wasn't just 'a stone' because it had arms, like a chair. And I rested my arms along them. I rested my arms along the arms of stone. And there was a kind of congruence.

Pause.

— Oh really?

— Yes. A kind of congruence – what, does that surprise you? – between the arms: the arms of stone, and the arms of . . .

— Flesh.

— What?

— Flesh.

— Exactly. Between the arms of stone and – yes – exactly – my arms of flesh. So – okay – I watched the trees. I'm watching the trees. And each tree is green, but each green is different. And in fact each *leaf* is different. Each leaf within each tree is of a different green. And they're all trembling. I mean each leaf is trembling, and the whole line isn't just bending, it's also waving. But ever so slightly. While the cold of the stone is – what – is seeping into me.

Pause.

Next thing I know I'm falling.

— You mean you're dreaming?

— Dreaming? No, I mean I'm falling. I mean that I am truly falling, that all of me is falling, towards the track.

Pause.

Then I woke up and this was over me.

— What was over you?

— This. This thing. This blanket was over me. I thought I had *died*. I thought, well okay, this is death.

Pause.

D'you have my watch?

— What?

— My watch. I was wearing a watch.

— Really?

— Yes. A gold watch.

— A gold watch.

— Yes. With a golden strap. A gold watch with a golden strap.

— It's on the table.

Rebecca goes to the table, letting the blanket fall. She slips on the watch, her back to Corinne.

— What is it you're looking at?

— I'm sorry?

— You're staring at me.

— We took the watch off. We thought you might damage it.

— Oh? We?

— My husband and I.

— My husband and I? (*faint laugh*)

— Where are you going?

— Can I get a glass of water through here?

— No. The other way.

— The other way.

— Yes. *That* way.

— The other way.

— Yes.

— *This* way?

  Pause.

  This way?

— Yes.

— Thank you.

— Through there.

— Well, thank you.

  Rebecca goes out.

— You'll need to turn on the light.

— Is there a light? I don't see it. Yes – okay – I see it.

A light goes on, spilling faintly into the room. We hear Rebecca at the tap. Light goes out. She reappears in the doorway with a glass of water, sips it.

What happened to my bag? It spilled?

— Yes?

— How did it spill?

— Out.

— It spilled out.

— Yes. Yes, I'm afraid it did.

— *(amused)* What? Was there a *scene*?

— A scene?

— What did I do? Did I make a scene? My god, how / embarrassing.

— You didn't do anything. You were asleep. There wasn't a scene.

— But the bag . . .

— The bag spilled out.

Rebecca calmly gathers her things and puts them back in the bag, keeping out a pack of cigarettes.
    Corinne watches her.

He isn't here.

— Who isn't here?

— My husband. He isn't here.

— You mean you're alone?

— What? Yes. No. No. I mean he's out.

— Where?

— Why?

— What? (*Slight pause.*) Why what?

— Do you ask?

— Where he is?

— Yes.

— Why do I ask where Richard is?

— Yes. You know his name.

— His name is Richard.

— I know his name is Richard.

— Where is he then?

— He's out. He's covering.

— He's covering?

— He's covering, yes, for / his partner.

— D'you have an ashtray?

— What? No. We don't. Sorry.

— Then is there something I may use?

— Use?

— Use as an ashtray.

— What d'you mean? Like a dish?

— Yes, like a dish. Like a plate. Like a . . .

— What, like a cup? A coffee cup.

— A dish, a cup, a coffee cup – or just a plate, just an ordinary / plate.

— No, I'm afraid there's nothing you can use as an ash-tray. We don't have anything you can use / as an ash-tray.

— No, you're right, it is disgusting. It is disgusting to wake in the night and to crave, my god yes, why do we immediately crave what will most do us harm? Coffee. A cigarette. Sex. (*faint laugh*) I'll just use the pack. I'll flick my ash right back into the pack.

She does so. Pause.

— Listen: there's something I have / to say to you.

— D'you mean Morris?

— I'm sorry?

— He's covering for Morris?

— Yes. Why? D'you know Morris?

— No, but I'd like to meet him. He sounds like a charac-ter.

— Oh yes, he's a character.

— You hate him?

— What?

— You hate Morris?

— (*faint laugh*) Is it / so obvious?

— Why do you hate Morris? *Completely* / obvious. Yes.

— Is it really that obvious?

— Well yes. You *hate* the man.

They both laugh.

Why do you hate Morris?

32

— You've never met him.

— No, but I'd like to. He reads Latin.

— What?

— Well doesn't he read Latin? Richard told me he / reads Latin.

— Yes, he reads Latin.

— Well then I'd like to meet him. I'd like to talk Latin with him. And history. I'd love to discuss history.

— You 'talk Latin' do you?

— Does that surprise you?

— No. Yes. Yes it does, actually. It does surprise me / very much.

— Oh really? Because I couldn't do what I do without Latin. I wouldn't *be* here without Latin.

— What *do* you do?

— What do I *do*? I study.

— You study.

— I study.

— You study Latin.

— I don't study Latin, no – I mean, yes, okay, I *study* it, but my *study*, what I study is History. And this is the place to be.

Pause.

If you're interested in History, then I guess this is the / place to be.

— I'm not interested in History.

33

— Everybody is interested in History.

— Perhaps where you come from. But I'm not. We're not. In fact, the opposite.

— The opposite?

— Yes.

— What opposite?

— That's not why we / came here.

— What opposite? Because the opposite of History is surely – forgive me – ignorance.

— That's not why we came here. We came here to live.

— To live.

— Yes. To live. Are you usually this / sententious?

— So you've not always lived in the country?

— What? No. Yes. *This* country? Yes.

— No. The country. Not *this* country. The country.

— The countryside.

— Yes. Okay. The countryside.

— No.

— Is that what you *call* it? The country*side*?

— No.

— Okay.

— It's the country. We call it the country.

— Okay. Good.

— *We* call it – I mean – the country, because we come from the town, but if you come from the country, then

34

you call it . . . I suppose you call it . . . (*faint laugh*) I don't know what you call it.

— Home.

— Yes. Perhaps.

— You would call it home.

— Why would you call it home? Do you come from the country?

— (*laughs*) Me? I come from the city. For me the city will always be home. I say to people 'back home', whereas for you . . .

— What?

— D'you say 'back home'?

— This is where we live. This is where our children will live. This *is* our home.

— Exactly. Well exactly: you and your children have nowhere to go / back to.

— This is our home. We don't want to 'go back'. We are a family. We are here permanently.

— And is that – what? – because of an ideal? Permanently. But how can you / be sure?

— What ideal? No. We just fell in love / with –

— You fell in love?

— Yes – with the house. I don't know what you / mean, 'ideal'.

— Well a rural – obviously – ideal. Virgil, for example, his ideal of the country. Of the harmonious . . . of the order of things, of the orderly cultivation of things. Of the tasks appropriate to winter and spring, summer and fall, the vines, the willow-beds, the . . . / almond trees.

— We simply came here to change our lives a little, to . . . and perhaps this sounds unreasonable – but yes, to be happier, to aim at any rate / to be

— No, not at all.

— happier. To get away – yes – permanently – from the city. It has nothing whatsoever to do / with Virgil.

— Not at all. To strive, you mean, to strive for your / family's happiness.

— If you *can* get away. Assuming that it is because I think that it is possible / to get away.

— The city makes people crazy.

— Yes.

— I've seen it. Crazy people. My *friends*.

— Yes.

— They don't sleep nights. They lie awake just listening, just listening to the city.

— Yes.

— But they're terrified. They're terrified to leave.

— I know. Are they? Yes.

— In case they miss – yes they *are* – in case they miss the opportunity, some opportunity which naturally may / never come.

— But we did, you see. We did get away. And when he showed me this house . . .

— I have some crazy friends. The stuff they do, the stuff they crave, you would / not believe.

— He showed me the house – this house – and that convinced me.

— He convinced you. He convinced you to come.

— Yes.

— He convinced you that this was good.

— It is good. It is good. I didn't need / to be convinced.

— The land. The stream. The beautiful house.

— Yes. The beautiful house. Why not?

Pause.

What do you want from me?

— Your . . . husband – almost killed me tonight. Back there on the track. Or did he not mention that? (*Lights cigarette.*) Oh man, that was something. That was quite something. That was a *hit*.

Pause.

I thought I had *died*. Or did he not mention that?

— Okay, okay, okay. Yes. Listen to me.

— Before he 'went out'. Before he 'went to cover'. Before he left me here without an ashtray.

— Listen to me.

— What? What? Yes? Listen? Okay. (*Slight pause.*) Well okay: I'm listening / to you.

— You've woken up in a strange house. I understand that you're confused. It's a big house. It's the middle of the night. I don't know you. I don't know what you want. I *do* know – and listen to me – I do know that his primary concern has been for your safety. Is that clear to you?

37

My husband is a doctor. You are in a doctor's house. You're an intelligent girl – a very – clearly – intelligent girl – but I will not accept – neither of us will accept – will not accept that you can simply accuse him of – where are you going?

Rebecca is getting up, putting her cigarettes back into the bag.

— I think I should leave. Intelligent girl? Fuck that. Fuck that. Why did he bring me here? He must've been totally out of it – out of his / fucking *mind*.

— You can't leave. No. There's nothing . . .

— Where is my / jacket?

— Please, there's nothing *out* there. There's no . . .

— I can't leave?

— . . . light. There's no . . . It's just *country*, there's no light or . . .

— I can't leave your / house? *What?*

— Of course you can leave the house, but not now, not while you're . . . Please be / sensible.

— Confused?

— Exactly.

— Because I'm not the one who is / confused.

— Not before we've talked.

— We have talked.

— Look: I just want to be honest with you, perfectly honest with you.

— You want to be honest?

38

— Yes. I'm / trying to –

— Because the more you talk, the less you say.

— That's not true. I'm / trying to . . .

— The less you really say.

— . . . to explain. No.

— You're trying to be / *honest*?

— All right, all right, all right.

Pause.

I'm asking you – which I realize I have perhaps no right to ask you – I realize, I realize – but asking you then to forget – appealing to you – may I? – to forget this error (which I'm sure it was) of judgement.

You don't *know* him. He's not . . .

Yes, he's a man, obviously, but he's not . . .

And perhaps – I don't know – but perhaps you gave him a sign, unwittingly gave him a sign which he mis-read. Which is no excuse – of course not – no. But maybe the sign – to him – d'you see? – who maybe can't read these signs – *because he is a man* maybe can't read these signs. Yes?

Pause.

His ignorance – yes – stupidity – yes, accepted. But to do you harm, I will not believe. No. I can't. A girl – a woman – a young woman accepts a ride from a man she's never met. And perhaps for her it's . . . I don't know what it is – it's a game? Is it a game? She's young – she's not afraid – she gets into his car – on a pretext – some pretext? – and however wrong this is – how-ever wrong *we* know this is – how does he (who is after all human) interpret that?

He's wronged you – clearly wronged you – and

39

you're angry – as you have every right to be – but then let *me* apologize. You will recover. For you it's just one afternoon, one night, from which you will soon recover. Whereas for us – and this is what I mean by honest – it's our life together – it's his whole position here – to speak quite frankly – that has been jeopardized.

Now if you need something – if you need . . . Because I don't know what you may want, what you may need – but if you need . . . / money, or –

— Just for an afternoon.

— What? Yes. I'm sorry if that / sounds blunt.

— (*quiet and intense*) But what d'you mean, 'just for an afternoon'? What d'you mean, 'a man she's never met'? Have you no inkling?

D'you really have no inkling?

And yet you condescend to me. You patronize me. With your house, your land, your children.

And accuse *me* of sententiousness?

Just for an afternoon?

He came to the country to *be with me*.

Yes.

Because of his longing to be with me.

Because of his greed to be with me.

'A man she's never met'? How can you *deceive* yourself? And then to *apologize* to me – on his behalf . . . (*faint laugh*) . . . in your own house?

Pause.

— I'd like you to leave.

— To touch my things – to take my things – to take / my *watch*.

— I said I'd like you to leave.

40

— The watch he gave me.

— Get out.

— But you wanted me to stay. I thought you wanted me to stay on account of my / confusion.

— I've changed my mind. I want you to leave. I want you to get out.

— Where can I go?

— I don't care where you go.

— Oh, shall I go to Morris?

Pause.

Shall I go to Morris? Shall I speak Latin? Shall I talk History?

(. . . paper)

IV

Same scene, later.
  Rebecca, alone.

— 'This song of husbandry . . . of crops and beasts and
  fruit trees I was singing while great Caesar was thun-
  dering beside the deep Euphrates in war, victoriously
  for grateful peoples.' Grateful peoples. (*faint laugh*)
  But what did *he* know? About crops. Or trees. How
  did he know that the 'peoples' were grateful?

  *Richard enters with a glass of water and gives it to
  Rebecca.*

  And how were the farms run? (Thank you.) I'll tell you
  how the farms were run. By slaves. By the labour of
  slaves. Which he neglects to mention.

— Please keep your voice down.

— But this is poetry. This is *pastoral.*

  Pause.
    She sips.

— So you've not seen Corinne?

— What? Your wife? (*Slight pause.*) I've already told you:
  I woke up. I was alone. In a strange house. I was
  afraid. So no: I have not / 'seen Corinne'.

— You haven't heard her move about?

— I've heard no one move about. I've heard nothing.
  Why would your wife / move about?

— If she was awake. If she was awake, she would move about.

Pause.

She would pace about.

— Can I take a shower? Where is it?

— No.

— Is it through here?

— No. You can't. You can't – I'm sorry – take a shower.

— Do I go through here?

— No, that's . . . that's . . .

— *What* is it?

Pause.

What is it?

— You don't go through there.

— Where do I go?

— You don't. It makes a noise.

— What noise?

— Yes.

— Does it?

— Yes. I'm sorry.

Pause.

— I won't make a noise.

— You *will* make a noise. I'm sorry, but you *will* make a noise.

— What noise? I won't / make a noise.

— The noise it makes. The noise of . . .

— Your shower makes a noise? What / noise?

— The noise of showering.

— Of what?

— Of showering. The noise of / the water.

— Your shower makes a noise of showering?

— Unfortunately, yes.

Pause.

— You mean the water?

— The water and also the curtain makes a noise on its track.

— What kind of noise?

— A kind of screeching, a kind of / screeching noise.

— I won't touch – well in that case I simply won't touch the curtain.

— It makes a / noise. No.

— I'll just shower.

— No. I'm terribly sorry. No.

Pause.

You'll wake my wife. You'll wake / the children.

— How will I do that? I can't / take a shower?

— *Listen* to me.

— I mean how exactly do you propose to . . . propose to . . . enforce . . .

— What?

— Enforce – yes – this prohibition?

— Please, I'm just / asking you.

— With violence?

— I'm just asking you not to use / the shower.

— With violence? Really?

— No. Listen. Let me explain. The shower – not with violence – the shower is up the stairs . . .

— Okay.

— You go up the stairs, but the shower is through –

— Thank you. So I go up the stairs.

— Yes. But no – no, you don't go up the stairs because what I mean is, is you have to pass through their room. The shower is through the children's room. Now do you see?

— It's through your children's room.

— Yes.

— I see. Your children.

— Yes.

— But why is that?

Pause.

Why is your house designed like that? Why do you pass through your children's room to reach / your bathroom?

— It's not a house.

— It's not a house?

— No, it's not a house, it's a . . .

46

— What is it?

— I'm telling you what it is. You know what it is. You know it's not a house, it's a granary, it's a . . .

— It's a granary.

— It *was* a granary. It was for grain. It was not a house. *Now* it's a house. And of course I'm not – you know I'm not – threatening you. I'm appealing – simply – d'you understand – appealing to your reason.

— But is this reasonable?

— Is what reasonable?

— This . . . route.

— Route.

— This strange – yes – route to your bathroom. Is this a reasonable route?

— I believe so. Yes. In fact it's always been a very good route – an ideal, you could call it, route.

— Until now.

— *Even* now.

— But not for me.

— Not – that's right – for you. Come on.

— What?

— Come on. We're going.

— We're going? Where?

— I'm taking you back.

— I don't trust you to take me back.

— Of course you trust me.

47

— Why should I trust you?

— I'm taking you back.

— Why should I trust you? You left me.

— I left you, yes, but I didn't *leave* you, and now I'm taking you back. I've *come* back, and I'm *taking* / you back.

— But this is my home.

— This is not – I'm sorry – your home.

— Then why did you bring me here?

— You know why / I brought you here.

— Was it to offer me a position?

— To do what?

— To offer me a position? To help your wife? To be the maid. Was it to be the maid?

— She doesn't need help. She's very capable.

— Get a maid. Fuck the maid.

— I don't want to fuck the maid.

— Everyone wants to fuck the maid.

— Well not me. In fact the opposite.

— The opposite? Really? (*faint laugh*)

— Yes really. Is that / funny?

— And what is the opposite of fucking the maid?

— The opposite of fucking the maid is not fucking the maid.

They both laugh quietly. She takes his hand.

— So where have you been?

— It was a baby.

— Oh, was it sick?

— No, it was born.

— Did you hold it?

— Of course I held it.

— Did the mother hold it?

— Yes.

— Did it cry?

— It screamed. Why?

— Was it beautiful?

— They found it beautiful.

— The parents.

— Yes, the parents found it beautiful. And so did I.

  Pause.

  The father thanked me.

— He thanked you?

— He put his arm around me.

— He was grateful.

— He was very grateful. I'd delivered his son.

— It was a boy.

— It was a baby boy. Yes.

— It was a family.

— It had . . . become one. He wanted me to have a drink with him . . .

— So you had a drink with him?

— . . . but I wouldn't.

Pause.

— You should've had a drink with him. The man has become / a father.

— But I wouldn't. I . . . he . . . followed me down the stairs . . . and he . . . trapped me in the hall. It was a very small hall. The electricity meter was screwed to the wall, and I could see the disc, the silver disc of the meter going round and round. He said to me, 'Drink, doctor?' And I must've looked completely blank, because he said it again. The disc was spinning, and I was thinking, how can such a small house use so much electricity? There must be something on – a fire – a freezer – drawing the current. 'I'm having one,' he said, 'what about you?' And he had a big . . . name on his shirt. The name of a brand. The name of the brand of shirt . . . *on* his shirt. He was so happy. He was so hopeful.

Pause.

— Well of course he was happy. You had delivered his son.

— But I said, 'No. I have to go. I have to work.'

— You disappointed him. He wanted to celebrate.

— No. That's just the thing. He looked relieved.

She grips his hand more tightly.

Don't hurt me.

— I'm not hurting you.

— I said: don't hurt me.

50

— What? Does that hurt?

— Yes. It hurts. Stop it. What is it?

— Really? Does that hurt?

— Yes.

He pulls his hand out of her grip. The tiny scissors drop to the floor.

You've cut my hand.

— I've what?

— You've made a hole in my hand.

— A hole in your hand?

— Yes.

— Oh my – you're angry.

— Yes.

— (*laughing*) You're so angry, Richard.

— Keep your voice down.

— I've made a hole in your hand? Is it deep? Are you in pain?

Pause.

Squeeze it.

— I'm squeezing it.

— Let me squeeze it.

— Don't touch me.

He allows her to take his hand.

— It's only the flesh.

— There *is* only flesh.

51

She sucks the wound, releases his hand.
He looks at her, smiles.

— What?

— There's blood on you.

— Where?

— Here on your face.

He touches her by the mouth.
She lets her fingers rest there a moment, then breaks away, and wipes her mouth on her sleeve.

— Can I see them?

— See what?

— Your kids?

— No. I've said.

— You've said?

— Yes. I've said.

— You've spoken.

— That's right.

Pause.

— What're their names?

— They don't have names.

— They don't have names.

— No.

Pause.

You know they don't have names. We have an agreement.

— I don't think we have an agreement any more.

— We have an agreement. Nothing's changed.

— Everything has changed. 'Nothing has changed'?
   What?

— They don't have names.

— For one thing, I'm *here*.

— No. You're wrong. You're not here.

— I'm not here?

— No.

— So where am I?

   Pause.

   I promise to tip-toe. Let me just tip-toe up and see. Let
   me just listen to them breathe. Or, if they're awake, I
   could tell them a story.

— They don't want to hear a story.

— But everyone wants to hear a story, don't they? I could
   say: Hello. I'm Rebecca. I'm the maid. Let me tell you
   a story. Would you like me to tell you a story? Oh yes
   please, Rebecca, tell us a story. Well once upon a time,
   children, there was a girl, there was a bright young
   girl, and she was sick, and she needed some medicine.
   So she went to a doctor and she said, doctor, doctor, it
   hurts, I need some medicine. But the doctor wouldn't
   give her any. He said, go away – don't waste my time –
   I have no medicine. So she went back again and she
   said, doctor, doctor, it really hurts, I need some medicine. And this time the doctor went to the door. He
   locked the door. He said: I need to take a history – roll
   up your sleeve. So she rolled up her sleeve and the doctor took a history. Then, children, he got one instru-

ment to look into her eyes. And another instrument to listen to her heart. And when he'd looked into her eyes and listened to her heart, he asked her to undress.

And when she'd undressed, he said: I see now how very sick you are – you need some medicine. She said: Doctor, am I going to die? He said: No, it's simply that your eyes are very dark and your skin is very pale. Your skin is so thin that when I touch it like this with my lips I can feel the blood moving underneath. You're sick, that's all. You need some medicine. So the treatment began.

The treatment was wild, children. It could take place at any time of day or night. In any part of the city. In any part of her body. Her body . . . became the city. The doctor learned how to unfold her – like a map.

Until one day the bright young girl decided the treatment would have to end – because the more medicine she took, the more medicine she craved – and besides, she was leaving for the country.

Now this made the doctor very angry. Because he'd broken all the rules – as he saw it – for her. Not just the kind of rules you children have – take off your shoes, wash your hands – but grown-up rules. Laws. He'd broken all these rules – these laws – and he was very angry. In fact he wept. You bitch, he said. You little bitch.

Because you see there'd been a terrible misunderstanding. Since the thing the bright young girl bitch called treatment, the doctor – who of course was sick himself – who craved medicine himself – imagined to be – what? – something personal. Something human. Which is why he followed her.

— Listen, listen, listen. Rebecca. What we need to –

— He followed her. He brought his / *family*.

54

— What we need to –

— Okay. Good. Yes. Tell me what / we need.

— Because there is a limit – not what we need – but don't you see there is a limit to what we . . .

— A limit?

— . . . to what we can – a limit, yes – usefully – tonight – don't you see – to what we can . . .

— Hope. Hope to achieve.

— Yes. No. No. To what we can . . . to what the two of us can . . . / *say*.

— Achieve in words.

— Yes, to what we can – exactly – achieve / in words.

— You see, I don't believe that. I think that is so totally / dishonest.

— I mean tonight, tonight when the two of us are . . .

— *I'm* not tired.

— . . . when we are – exactly – tired – so tired that we / can't think.

— Because I refuse to believe that. There's not a limit to what can be said, only a limit to how honest we are prepared to be. *I'm* not tired. *I* / can think.

— Well I am. You've been sleeping. I've been working. I've / been driving.

— So tell me what it is you think / we can't say.

— I've been working. I'm not prepared to have / this conversation.

— Not prepared? Just tell me.

— Tell you what?

— Just tell me what it is you think we can't say.

— How can I tell you what I can't – I *beg* your pardon? – say? *What?*

— Exactly. Well exactly. Because there is / *no such thing*.

— (*softly*) I should've left you on the fucking track.

— What?

— I should've left you on the fucking track.

— Left me?

— And that is the truth. *Left* you there.

— You mean for dead?

— I mean – yes I do – for dead.

> *Pause.*
> *Rebecca begins to laugh.*

— You know she thought I had given you a sign? (*Slight pause.*) Your wife. She thought I had given you 'a sign'. She wanted to apologize for you. Isn't that cool? (*Slight pause.*) She's actually quite attractive. Why did you always say how unattractive she was? How you had to turn the light out? (*Slight pause.*) You / lied to me.

— You've talked to her.

— You lied to me. What? Yes. Well yes, certainly I talked to her. (*Slight pause.*) Oh, don't worry. She's gone. Some while ago. She took the kids and left. (*Slight pause.*) They were so sleepy. And the way she bundled them. My god, the way she bundled them out.

> *Pause.*
> *They don't move.*

Don't hurt me.

— I'm not hurting you.

Pause.
  He looks at her.

— Then don't look at me.

— I'm not looking at you.

— Then don't look at me.

They stare at each other.

(. . . scissors)

V

Two months later.

Sunday morning. The same space, but transformed by daylight.

A huge window looks out on to the countryside.

Corinne is opening envelopes. She takes out the cards, reads them, lays them down in a pile.

Richard enters with a glass of water as she opens the last card – his – which is why she turns and says:

— Thank you.

— D'you like it?

— D'you *mean* this?

— Do I . . . what? . . . mean? Sorry?

— (*laughing*) This. *This.*

— Well look, I'm a doctor, I'm not a . . . I don't pretend to be a . . . / *writer.*

— What you've written. But what you've written here – d'you mean this?

— Yes. Well yes I do. Of course I mean what / I've written.

— Thank you.

— What?

— *Thank* you.

— It's a promise.

— Will you keep it?

— What?

— I said will you / keep it?

— I am keeping it. You *know* I'm keeping it.

— Keeping yourself clean.

— Keeping myself – yes – extremely clean.

Both smile. She takes the water from him. Pause. Then she takes a sip.

The stream will be swollen. We needed rain. Everything's green. I mean everything that should be green – is green. It was extraordinary.

— What was?

— The downpour. The rain in the night.

— What rain?

— The rain in the night.

— What rain / in the night?

— We listened to it. It rained and rained. It was the most extraordinary downpour.

— I think I was asleep.

— You were definitely awake.

— Was I?

— You know you were. We both were.

— I don't remember any rain.

— But you remember being awake. I hope. You turned to me.

— I turned to you?

— Well someone turned to me.

— (*faint laugh*) Yes.

— You remember *that*. I hope.

— Yes.

   Pause.

   Yes, I remember that. (*She smiles.*)

— And it rained. We talked about it.

— Oh? What did we say?

— Just . . . 'it's raining'. Just . . . 'listen to the rain'.
Things like that. We said how green everything would
look, how swollen the stream would be.

— I think I was asleep. I think I fell straight asleep.

— You said how funny it would be if the house was
washed away.

— Me? Did I? I thought I fell / straight asleep.

— We talked and talked. You didn't fall straight asleep.
We lay there talking.

— Perhaps I was just pretending.

— Pretending what?

— To be awake. Perhaps I was just pretending to be
awake.

— How can you pretend to be awake?

— *I* don't know.

   They both laugh.

   Maybe I'm doing it now.

— Pretending.

— Yes.

— You're very good at it.

— Thank you.

— No one would ever know.

— I know they'd never know.

— It's the way you open your eyes.

They both laugh. She drinks some water.

How is the water?

— How is the water?

— Yes.

— Delicious. Cold. Why?

— What does it taste of?

— Taste of? Nothing.

— Really?

— Why? What should it / taste of?

— You used to think it had a taste. When we first came here. It worried you.

— (*laughs*) What did?

— (*laughs*) The taste of the water. The taste of the water worried you.

— The taste of the water worried me? What did it taste of?

— It didn't taste of anything.

— Then why did it worry me? It doesn't worry me now.

— Good.

— Well does it you?

— It never did worry me. It always . . . delighted me. I like to think of the rain seeping through the rock. Then welling up at the spring. Don't you?

— I've never really thought about it.

— Can I get you some more?

— What?

— Can I get you some more / water?

— I've still got this to drink.

She drinks the rest of the water. He takes the glass. She begins to laugh.

— What? What is it? What?

— It's just that you're being so . . .

— Am I? What?

— So . . . solicitous.

— Really?

— Yes.

— Solicitous.

— Yes.

— What does that mean?

— Don't you know what / it means?

— Well tell me then what it means. No, I don't. I've / no idea.

— To care. It means to care.

— Okay.

— Don't you believe me? (*Slight pause. They both laugh.*)

Why are you looking at me like that? Don't you /
believe me?

— No, it's just that I have in my mind, why do I have in
my mind, because I have in my mind that it's about sex.

— Sex? No. Nothing to do / with sex.

— Paying in fact for sex.

— It means to care – to be caring. That is 'solicit'. You
mean solicit – to . . . / solicit someone.

— You mean like a solicitor.

— No, I don't mean like a solicitor.

They both laugh.

— But it's not wrong is it?

— What? To pay for sex?

— To care. It's not wrong of me to care.

— About what?

— About you.

— I don't know.

— You don't know? You mean it's wrong?

— I don't know.

Pause. She fiddles with the cards, looks up, smiles.

No – of / course not.

— You should put up your cards.

— What? I don't want to.

— Yes. Stand them up. Stand them all up. Put them / in a
row.

64

— I don't want to. It will make me feel old.

— But you're not old.

— (*faint laugh*) Why d'you keep looking at me / like that?

— Old? You're not old. And I'm looking at you – if I am indeed 'looking at you' – precisely because you're not old. You look – you still look like a girl.

— (*laughs*) What 'girl'?

— (*laughs*) *Like* a girl. Not *what* girl. Like / a girl.

— (*laughs*) I don't want to look like a girl. What if I don't want to look like a girl? Where are you going?

— To get something.

— I don't want any more water.

— That's not what I'm getting.

— What are you getting then?

— (*humorously*) Ah-*ha*.

He goes out, taking the empty glass. She looks through the cards.

— D'you know what I was thinking – because I was opening these and I was thinking I'd like someone to 've died and there to be a big cheque.

— (*off*) What?

— A cheque. A big cheque.

— (*off*) Who do you know who could've died?

— Anyone I know could die. People do die. My parents. My parents are a perfect example of people who / could die.

— (*off*) Your parents – I'm terribly sorry – but your parents are not / going to die.

— I would like my parents to have collided with the side of a mountain in South America and there to be no survivors. That way it would be painless and they would stop sending me cards with puppies on them / every year.

— (*off*) You can't say that.

— I can't say puppies? What are you doing / in there?

— (*off*) You can't say that about / your parents.

— I can say what I like about / my parents.

— (*off*) You have money. You don't need money. You live in a big house / in the country . . .

— Not real money. Not the kind of money some / people have.

— (*off*) . . . and your parents have nothing. If they *were* to die – and I'm sure it would be in agony –

— (*laughs*) Don't.

— (*off*) Yes. The utmost – knowing them – (*He reappears, holding a parcel.*) – deliberate agony. Then you would receive nothing.

— I'd probably get a bill.

— You would in fact – yes – get a bill.

— A big bill.

— You'd be left with nothing.

— Less than nothing.

— Just the memory of their agony.

— Don't.

— You'd be left with the memory of their agony and a bill for repatriating their remains. From wherever.

— I know.

— From Chile.

— Don't.

— Or Peru.

— (*smiles*) What's this?

— It's for you. It's a present.

— I don't need a present.

— Of course you need a present. Open it.

— What is it?

— Open it.

Pause. She starts to unwrap it.
Inside the wrapping paper is a cardboard box. Inside the box is a pair of shoes.
The shoes appear quite sober and elegant, but at the same time there is something unsettling about them – and this may not be apparent until Corinne puts them on. Perhaps, for example, they are a little too high for her.

— Thank you.

— D'you like them?

— They look very expensive.

— They are very expensive. Put them on.

She puts them on.

— How did you know my size?

— I don't know your size. I took a shoe.

— You took a shoe?

— I took a shoe – yes – to the shoe shop.

She stands up.

— Like the Prince.

— What?

— Like / the Prince.

— That's right. In a fairy-tale. How do they feel?

— I don't know.

— Aren't they comfortable?

— They're very comfortable.

— Then what do you mean?

— I'd need to walk in them.

— Well walk in them then.

She walks. She turns. She smiles.

— So?

— You look . . . transformed.

— (*laughs*) Transformed? Into what?

— Don't you like them?

— It's strange.

— What is?

— To be given things.

— It's normal to be given things.

— Yes.

— It's perfectly normal, Corinne, to be given things.

— Yes. Is it?

— Well of course it is. You know it is. They suit you.

— Do they?

— Very much. You look quite different.

— Is that what you want?

— What? Yes. No. I just want you to be happy.

— Well I am happy.

— That's all I want.

— Well I am happy.

Slight pause. She walks again in the shoes, turns and smiles.

— I can take them back. I can change them. *You* can change them. We can go together and / change them.

— Don't do that. Why do that?

Phone.

— You don't like them.

— I love them. Really. Thank you. (*She picks up phone.*) Hello?
  Sophie. Hi. Good morning. How are they? Did they sleep?
  (*Laughs.*) Really? Really? Well that's marvellous.
  No, it's a treat, it's a real birthday treat. You've been so –
  No, you've been really kind to us.
  Well . . . Richard made me breakfast . . . Yes, and then I opened my cards . . . Yes, and then I opened my present.

Shoes. He's given me a pair of shoes.

Yes. Lovely. I'm wearing them now. Apparently I look transformed.

I don't know. They make me feel rather . . .

— (*kissing the back of her neck*) Decadent.

— (What?)

— Decadent. They make you feel / decadent.

— (*laughs*) He's telling me I'm decadent. (Stop. I'm talking to Sophie.)

— Deeply decadent.

— Nothing. Sorry. He's just being a little . . . (You're distracting me. Stop.) He's just being a little . . . stopping me from / talking.

— (*moving away*) Ask her, did she find the money?

— Very typical, I'm afraid. (What?) Excuse me, Sophie. (What?)

— Did she find the money?

— (What money?) Hello? Yes. Nothing, it's just / Richard, he –

— The money I put in the cup.

— He's asking me if you found the money he put / in the cup.

— I put some money – that's all – in the cup.

— (She says you shouldn't have.) Well of *course* you should be paid.

— I just wondered if she's / found it.

— A mistake? What kind of mistake?

As Sophie explains, Corinne bends over and slips off the shoes.

Uh-huh . . . uh-huh . . . Really? Well if that's what he gave you, then I assume that's what he meant / to give you.

— I felt generous. I thought she might like to go out and / buy something.

— (*laughs*) I'm sure he didn't mean to *frighten* you – he was just being generous.

— Frighten her? Of course I didn't mean to / frighten her.

— Of *course* you should keep it. You're *meant* to keep it.

— She has to keep it.

— You have to keep it, Sophie. Now listen: do tell them that mummy –
    That's right: tell them that mummy and daddy are . . .

— Coming to get them after tea.

— Are . . . missing them very much and coming to get them after tea.
    Okay.
    Thanks, Sophie. (*Hangs up.*) Why did you give her so much money? She said she was terrified.

— By what?

— By all that money.

— By me?

— No. By all that money. Not by you. She likes you.

— How can you tell?

— You can just tell. Her voice changes.

— What d'you mean: she likes me?

— I just mean she likes you. Her voice changes when she uses / your name.

— You mean I flirt with her?

— I mean she flirts with *us*. Takes our children. Scrubs our floors. Asks for nothing.

— That's because she despises us. It's because she despises you and me and everything we stand for.

— Well she has a very strange way of showing it and I don't think we 'stand' for anything. People don't 'stand' for things, they . . .

— People don't stand for / things.

— . . . exist.

— What?

— They exist, they simply exist. Perhaps what you mean to say is that you despise your*self*.

— (*laughs*) Why should I despise myself?

— (*laughs*) Well *I* don't know. I don't know why you should despise yourself. Okay, she's poor, but she has a cottage, she has a . . .

— Telephone.

— A telephone, a cooker . . . So why do I have to *feel* something? Please don't ask me to / *feel* something.

— I'm not asking you to feel anything.

— Because I don't. I can't.

Silence.

— You know what I was thinking: I was thinking that perhaps we could change the . . .

72

— Change the what?

— The design – the design, actually, of the house. I've been thinking about upstairs, particularly / about upstairs.

— What's wrong with upstairs? I like upstairs. I like this house. I don't want / to change it.

— I'm not saying I don't like the house, I'm just saying perhaps we could change one or two things.

— Upstairs.

— Yes. Well yes – because the way it's arranged / isn't logical.

— Whose idea is that?

— Sorry?

— Why isn't it logical? Why should it be / logical?

— Whose *idea*? No one's. Mine. My idea.

— Morris's? Is it Morris's idea?

— To change the house? Morris?

— (*laughs*) Yes. Given his / thirst for control.

— (*laughs*) Of course not. *What* did you say?

— (*laughs*) His thirst – yes – for control.

— His thirst.

— Yes. Well surely you've noticed. Don't tell me that after all this time you still haven't noticed his thirst / for control.

— His thirst for control? Listen, I'm just talking about changing one or two things upstairs, that's all. The layout upstairs. Which is nothing whatsoever to do I can

73

assure you with Morris. Morris has been very good to us.

— Of course.

— To both of us.

— Yes. He lied.

— He defended my judgement. He did not / lie.

— Exactly. He lied. You left a man to die and Morris lied for you.

Pause. Corinne begins to laugh.

— (*smiles*) What?

— Oh god, I thought you'd lost your sense of humour. I thought, oh no, he's finally lost his famous sense of humour.

— But in fact you were wrong.

— In fact I was wrong.

— In fact my famous sense of humour survives intact.

— In fact your famous sense of humour does – remark-ably – survive / intact.

— So. Listen. What shall we do? Shall we go out?

— What?

— Go out. Let's drive somewhere. Let's get out the map.

— Okay.

— We could visit the Wall. We could have a picnic.

— Okay.

— Because we live in the country and we never . . .

— I know.

— We never . . .

— Exactly. You're right.

— . . . experience . . .

— It's true.

— . . . experience those things.

— The Wall.

— The Wall. The Fell.

— You mean walk along the Wall.

— Walk along the Wall. Walk the Fell. Why have we never walked along / the Wall?

— Have we really never walked along the Wall?

— Never.

— I could wear my shoes, then.

— What?

— I could wear my shoes.

— I don't think so.

— Oh, don't you think so?

— It's wet.

— Is it?

— It rained.

— Did it?

  Pause.

— Is something wrong?

— No, nothing's wrong.

75

— Let's go out then.

— I've *been* out.

— I don't think so.

— I think I have.

— When was that?

— Yesterday evening. I went on a trip.

— What trip?

— You took the children to Sophie's, and I went on a trip, that's all.

— You didn't tell me.

— Oh, didn't I tell you? Not in the night?

— No.

— I thought we talked. I thought we talked and / talked.

— What trip?

Pause.

What trip?

— Why?

— I'd like to know.

— You'd like to know what I did with my evening.

— Well yes – yes, I would like to know what you did with your / evening.

— You'd gone. I locked up. I crossed the yard. I got into my car. I twisted the mirror. I looked at myself.

Pause.

— How did you look?

76

— Complicit.

— Show me.

— (*smiles*) What?

— Show me how you looked.

— I looked complicit.

— Show me.

She looks down – seems about to try – but then laughs.

— I can't.

— Can't you do it?

— Not if I don't feel it.

— Oh, don't you feel it?

— No. Complicit? No. Why / should I?

— But why did you twist the mirror? Tell me.

— Oh, to reverse. I needed to reverse – or no – not needed
– but I did – reverse. Reversing gave me enormous
pleasure. Watching the house as it shrank gave me the
most enormous pleasure. It got so small so quickly. I'd
backed out on to the road before I knew it, and the
house smiled back at me through the trees.

Pause.

— So *you* were smiling.

— Well yes – I must've been. (*She smiles.*) Probably
because the evening was so perfect. So light.

— You mean the sun was nowhere near setting.

— The sun – that's right – was nowhere near setting and
the moon was up. It was flecked – this will amuse you
– like an egg.

— What kind of egg?

— Like a grey egg.

— What kind of egg?

— Well, a bird's egg, / obviously.

— So then you began to drive.

— What?

— So then you began / to drive.

— So then I began – yes, obviously – to drive away from the house. I turned right at the fingerpost and the road was so utterly long and straight I knew it must be old. I knew it must be nothing to do with me, this road, this old road. I didn't really like it being old. I didn't really like it being straight. Because after all I'd gone for an aimless drive and now – well – you can imagine – this road was coercing me. So when it ran out, I was pleased. It stopped at a ditch. No sign – just a ditch.

Pause.

— So that was the end of your little trip. That's what you did with your evening. Drove to a ditch.

— What? No. I got out of the car – oh no, my trip was just beginning – I got out of the car and I leapt across the ditch.

— (*laughs*) You leapt across the ditch.

— (*laughs*) Yes. Like a mad thing. And I began to run up the hill. You should've seen me running up that hill. I thought: I haven't run like this for no reason since I was a girl. Everything flapped – my hair . . . my clothes . . .

— You weren't dressed for the country.

— No. I had utterly failed to dress for the country. My dress was flapping round my legs like a flag and I knew I should go back to the car but I knew I wouldn't go back to the car.

— Why wouldn't you go back to the car?

— BECAUSE I DIDN'T WANT TO GO BACK TO THE CAR. (*quietly*) I didn't want to go back to the car, not now I had discovered the track.

It wasn't at all what I'd imagined, not the hard thin sheep or goat track I'd imagined. No, it was . . . broad, and littered with shale. At least, I think it was shale. It made a noise as I walked, a kind of clatter. And that's when I realized, as I slithered and clattered my way along the shale, that there was nothing human.

Well *I* was there, obviously. *I* was human, but nothing else was. I looked out for human things. Because I thought I might see – you know – a piece of wire or a spent cartridge with the top blown out. I thought I might see a plastic bag snagged in a hedge. Only there was no hedge. I thought I might see a needle or a piece of brick. I longed – you know – to see something human like a needle, or a piece of brick mixed with the shale. Or to hear – even to hear something human other than myself. Other than my feet. Other than my heart. A plane. Or children screaming. Only there was nothing. Not even a track now. Because the track – just like the road – stopped. Or it . . . what did it do? . . . it 'gave out'.

The track – that's right – gave out, and now there were just . . . clumps. Which meant, of course, stepping – although I needn't – but stepping from one clump to the next. You should've seen me stepping the way a child steps from one clump to the next until I reached the stone. Well I say 'the stone', but the stone had arms, like a chair. So you could sit . . . within the

79

stone. You could rest your arms along the arms of the stone, and from within the stone, look out at the land.

Pause.

— And how was the land?

— Oh, the land was lovely. But the stone was cold. I don't think the sun had ever warmed it. I was afraid it would stick to my skin, like ice. And then Morris appeared.

— Morris? What did he want?

— Well that's what I said. I said, 'What is it, Morris? What do you want?' He said, 'I've been following you for hours. Didn't you hear me calling you? You dropped this.'

— Dropped what?

— Well that's what I said. I said, 'Dropped what, Morris? Just what have I dropped?' 'Your watch, of course,' he said. And he dangled it in front of my face from its golden strap, so I could see all its tiny works. I said, 'I'm afraid you're mistaken. It's very beautiful, but it's not mine. It's very delicate, but it isn't mine.' Which is when I noticed – and this will amuse you – that the stone had started to devour my heart.

Pause.

— Oh really?

— The stone had started to devour my heart. Yes. Why? Does that surprise you? I said to Morris, 'Morris. Help me. This stone is devouring my heart.' Only I didn't say it like that, softly like that. I said it like a mad thing. Which is why, I suspect, he gripped my shoulders to establish a certain authority. And when he'd established a certain authority, he said, 'It's only a stone. There's no need to shriek. How could a stone do that?' I said, 'I don't know, Morry, I thought perhaps you would be able to tell me.' He said, 'Are you afraid?' I said, 'Well yes, Morry, of course I'm afraid. I don't seem able to move and this stone is devouring my heart. When I get up from this stone, what if my heart has gone? What if I have to spend the rest of my life simulating love?'

The phone rings.

And Morris said, 'I'm sure you simulate love very well. I'm sure the two of you will simulate love immaculately.' (*faint laugh*) He's a character.

— Am I not, then?

— Not what?

— Am I not a character?

— Oh yes – you're a character – very definitely a character – but quite a different character. Kiss me.

The phone continues to ring.

— I have kissed you.

— Then kiss me again.

Neither moves. The phone continues to ring.

(. . . stone)